CW00401182

Communicating Through Change

Lessons Learned From Real Life

by
Alicia Sedgwick

Embrace change with acceptance,
acknowledgement and recognition to learn, grow
and move forward to a stronger you

Legal Title Publication Page

Author: Alicia Sedgwick, The Communications Guru
www.aliciasedgwick.com

Literary Agent and Editor: Wendy Yorke, WRITE. EDIT. PUBLISH
www.wendyyorke.com

Publisher: Serapis Bey Publishing, www.parulagrawal.com

Front Cover Image: Photographer, Mike Colquhoun

ISBN 978-1-7356711-6-1

Dedications

Through the many changes in my life, I was blessed to have the most incredible parents who taught me that life is to be lived to the fullest. They gave me confidence, joy and an appreciation of life. This book is dedicated to them.

It is also dedicated to my beloved spouse, the most wonderful and amazing support and certainty in any waves of change and instability. She is my motivation, inspiration and the love of my life.

"Depicting her life as a woman in a changing society, Alicia gives us insights about how to heal past and current struggles, which each one of us has faced or could be facing. As her life unfolds, the reader is guided to better understanding their own emotions. Thus, providing comfort in knowing that we are not alone on this self-empowerment journey."

Audrey Dossou, 19, chemical engineer student, Canada

"I love the way we can dip in and out of this helpful, practical and touching book and read the chapters most relevant to us in that moment. It was a real comfort to me and reads as though you are talking with Alicia and she knows you. I definitely took many good lessons from this book and I loved the way the chapters were sectioned into What I have learned etc. Great structure, congratulations."

Justine John, Author, United Kingdom

About The Author

Alicia Sedgwick began her career as a lawyer, specialising in family law. This was her first step in helping people who were experiencing difficult changes in their lives. When she moved to the South of France, she began working in radio, as well as in event management, taking care of talent and celebrities. She also created her own internet television show, *Asking Alicia*, to help families dealing with impactful issues and the profound changes those challenges brought with them.

Alicia began teaching at the International University of Monaco in Public Speaking and Presentation Skills, Leadership and Managing People. Her communications courses are based on her belief that when you can communicate effectively and with impact, you will be successful in your professional and personal relationships. Soon, her training was extended to the International School of Monaco, and for businesses, individuals, associations and corporations. She is currently helping people to be brilliant online, where communications are so focused in this Covid climate. Alicia is also a professional MC for events, such as TEDxMonteCarlo, where she brings her individual talent of making everyone feel embraced, included and involved, with humour and empathy.

Hailed as The Communications Guru by her global followers, Alicia specialises in training and coaching for all age groups and backgrounds. She develops her international student's communications skills and builds their confidence, as well as empowering, motivating and inspiring them. She also helps people navigate their way through the challenges that life throws at us, with the backing and support of Team Alicia, which she created for her students as a place where they can go to feel cared for and nurtured. This book is her opportunity to share more of herself and tell her story to help more people with their lives. She knows from her life experiences that when we share our story and communicate effectively through change, we can be stronger people and make a more significant contribution in the world.

Change Challenges

"The one thing we can be sure of – in this life – is that there will be change."

This is a truth I have never wanted, or liked and yet my life has been full of it. In this collection of chapters of my personal experiences, specifically related to change, I hope you will learn from my experiences to deal with your own and to be able to also share your story. As you dip in and out of the chapters, you may feel that the experience is not relevant to you right now. However, I trust when you return to the book, a certain story will be highly pertinent for you in that moment.

A dear friend reminded me recently how I had agonised about changing my job from one legal partnership to another; spending hours deliberating on the decision; and talking and talking about it! I have always found it difficult to let anyone, or anything go. But I have had to learn to deal with change in my life and to adopt a different approach, which is what

I share with you in this book. I provide you with my life learnings about managing and communicating through each change and challenge that life throws at us all, so you can benefit from the best result for you, each time.

Wherever you are in your life, this book provides you with an insight into my life; sharing with you what I have learned and showing you how you can deal with your experiences of change, coming through them with strength and courage. It provides you with practical guidance and applicable exercises to enable you to take conscious actions that will help you communicate your way through a variety of different changes. While the chapters can be read in isolation, the exercises can be applied to more than one change challenge. This book will also help you to understand that you are not alone and whenever you face these challenges, there is support from the insight shared here. Plus, the opportunity to belong to Team Alicia, a supportive group of like-minded people where you are free to be yourself without inhibition, worry, anxiety or fear. Where you will not be judged; you will be nurtured and cared for and what is said and shared in Team Alicia, stays in Team Alicia!

Welcome to communicating your way through your life's change challenges, with understanding and empowered to be authentically you!

Chapter 1
RELATIONSHIPS

"What I have learned is … that you cannot live a falsehood."

I remember sitting in my childhood bedroom in my Mum and Dad's house in St Davids Drive, Leigh-on-Sea in England, the night before my wedding and asking Mum why was I doing this? We completed a list of pros and cons that evening, but the next day I was married.

I also remember the day after the wedding when we returned to that same house to open our wedding gifts with family and friends who were there to celebrate with us, and how I did not want to leave for our honeymoon later that day. I recall crying in a telephone box (no mobile telephones then!) to Mum and Dad, saying that I wanted to come home on the first night of my honeymoon!

Great start to wedded bliss?! Did I love my husband? Yes. Was I in love with my husband? No. Did I like my husband? Not particularly! Would I have chosen him as my friend? No. But it was the conventional thing to do. He was the most persistent suitor and the best one to care for me, support me financially and give us both a life of security. For the next seven years, I did what my head told me to do and not my heart or gut. Until, I could not stand being untrue to myself any longer. Until, I could not face another day of living a lie.

Before that I had felt the maternal urges of wanting a family and cementing the conventional life we had created. The talk began of our wishes for children and our life with them. That was when the cracks began to really show in our relationship. My idea of a life shared with family and friends, our children blissfully in the arms of my parents and their love and warmth did not correspond with my husband's ideal of a home in a remote part of the country, with a moat around it and drawbridge to keep out everyone else.

Finally, I confronted the elephant in the room. I was not happy and I was sure I was not making him happy. Indeed, that was so. He was prepared to bury his head in the sand and let it go on. I was not. The parting and separation happened. At first, it was amicable, if not emotional and then it dissolved into acrimony because sadly, these matters so frequently do. We say things that cannot be taken back. Then, it was divorce and I was a family lawyer who knew only too well how these situations can unfold. However, I was not prepared for the pain and the friendships that fell by the wayside. For my Mum, the horror of my being financially insecure was terrible and as a result, her worry caused me to feel concern and remorse. But, for all of the disruption in having to stand on my own two feet in every way, I was also hugely liberated. Free to be me at last! Change, which I instigated, admittedly.

However, when you do not feel happy, contented, peaceful, authentic, fulfilled or satisfied in your relationship and you are not living in accordance with your values and goals, you need to step away, or seriously discuss your feelings with your spouse or partner. Maybe, they feel the same way, but have not had the courage to tell you! See if you can work through it. Talk to each other, after you have had a good talking to yourself!

When you live your life for someone else, or when you think society directs you to live in a certain way, or you live to please anyone other than yourself, then you will not be happy. You will not be true to yourself; you will not, therefore, be true to other people; and ultimately, not only will you suffer mentally and physically, you will also cause more pain and hurt for other people. It is not easy being your authentic self, but it is essential for a happy and successful life.

However, when you are your true self - no matter what obstacles life throws at you - it is possible to find a way around them and reframe them because you are you, honestly and truthfully. You are following your heart, head, soul and listening to the pit of your stomach, where you – actually - feel every falsehood.

What I have learned is … how critical it is in life to love yourself! It sounds trite, but before you can love anyone else and enjoy a good relationship, you first need to love and value yourself. When your relationships with other people do not enhance your life, bringing you joy, support, laughter and understanding then, think carefully about why you are with that person. Are you being honest with yourself, as well as your partner or spouse? Is your partner or spouse being honest with themselves and you? Can you discuss your feelings and the relationship gaps you feel? Can you consult with a counsellor to help both of you to be honest and real? Can you go to a mediator to resolve issues in an amicable way, as soon as possible?

Stepping away from a relationship is not easy, especially if you have children, and/or financial concerns together. However, when you know in your heart and soul that you are living a life which is a lie, and is not in accordance with your deepest and highly-valued beliefs then, first talk with your partner or spouse. Or seek out guidance from an external objective expert, a counsellor for example, to help give you the strength to walk away, or to repair any gaps in your relationship. Or, consult with a lawyer to establish the practical steps to make your move.

Balance Exercise

Step 1. Make a list of all your pros and cons - for and against - why you are in the relationship that is concerning you.

Step 2. Consider and weigh up, which list comes up with the most points. For, or against? Be really honest with yourself.

Step 3. When the list is mostly 'for' the relationship, then you need to look at the 'against' list and see how these aspects can be worked on and sorted out. Ask yourself the following questions and be totally honest with yourself when you answer them from your heart.

- Are there solutions to resolve these issues?
- Is it worth saving my relationship because these aspects far outnumber not being in the relationship?
- Can I talk to my partner or spouse and express the difficulties I am experiencing in our relationship?

- Can I show them my list?

- Maybe, they have their own list that they want to discuss with me?

- Maybe, I will see a pattern emerging or that our differences are too wide to resolve?

- Maybe, they are closer than I think and we can actually work on them together; understanding that we both want to be together, but we have lost sight of how this can be achieved?

Step 4. When the list is mostly 'against' the relationship, you need to look carefully at the issues and consider if they can be resolved by counselling or seeking other external expert help.

- Always firstly, talk with your partner or spouse and explain how you are feeling and give them the opportunity to respond. When the issues are too profound, consult with a lawyer to find out the practical implications of separating.

- An alternative action is that you could write to your partner or spouse because sometimes it is too hard to speak face-to-face. Write down how you feel. Send that to your partner or spouse and explain that you want to be able to talk with them about it, if they want to, as well. If they do not and they do not respond with empathy to your letter, you may have the answers that this exercise is giving you the chance to receive!

Affirmations

I am not hanging onto anyone who is not enabling me to be truly me.

My relationships enhance my life and are a joy to share.

Chapter 2
IDENTITY: FACING THE TRUTH ABOUT YOUR SEXUALITY

"What I have learned is … that it is nobody else's business who we love, or live with, and we are free to be ourselves. We must listen to our intuition and our inner voice when it speaks the truth of our identity and we must not suppress that message."

I always felt more comfortable around girls. Apart from my brother and some of my cousins, most boys and men were threatening. I did not like their overwhelming desire for sex or being physical. I did not like their misinterpretation of my affectionate, demonstrative nature as being flirtatious and sexual. As a young girl, I played the game of talking about boys and going out with boys, but what I really enjoyed was the time spent with my girlfriends. I enjoyed supporting them with their love lives and helping them develop their relationships with their chosen male partners.

I remember hating leaving my infant school teacher to go into another class and leaving my secondary school teacher whose house I cycled around to catch a glimpse of her. Also, I had a crush on my female French teacher, who I adored and hated that she was married to the male science teacher! There were not the words for these feelings when I was growing up, except those spoken in hushed tones, or disparaging ones. The truth was that from the start, I liked women.

Then, I fell in love with a woman at work and I knew that all the feelings I had put aside for being the 'right thing to do' in the eyes of society and my parents, were my true feelings. All the pain and the joy, all the bliss and the romance, these were my reality but they were not my real life. Later, when I was in love again with another woman, I knew that I could not go on living the lie.

However, when I was first divorced and free to be truly me, my Mum said to me "People can think what they like but they need never know." The message to me was to maintain the facade of conventional life - albeit as a single woman – but not to live outwardly as gay. Was it better? Yes, and no. I understood that it was not anyone's business how I loved, or who I loved. I understood privacy. I understood that my parents concern for me at being ridiculed and losing out on opportunities was genuine. Yet, it was hard to comprehend that - in this day and age - all that was true.

Eventually, moving to live in France with my beloved Annette, it was important to me that I was no longer hiding in any way. I was determined that right from the start, my life from then on was to be totally open and I could truly be me. Fortunately, Annette felt the same way! It is such a joy to be married to the woman I love and adore, and to receive positive support from everyone around us. We share an equal and balanced relationship. Most people who know us, love to be with us because they feel the ease that we have with each other; the deep love and understanding. It is a profound blessing to be in a relationship where we are true to ourselves and each other, and not to experience any negative reactions from anyone.

What I have learned is … how important it is to listen to yourself. Listen and accept that inner voice which speaks to you. Know when and where you feel comfortable and at ease with yourself. You deserve to be true to yourself, always. Seek out like-minded people who understand you and can support you. It is not right that you should feel afraid of being you, whether gay, straight, male, female, intersex, non-binary, transgender, and/or bisexual. When you are afraid because of the environment you live in, find the strength - with the help of your tribe of people or community - to move away from it, if possible. There are many organisations who can help you if you do, such as Micro Rainbow in the United Kingdom, for example. There are many other people exactly like you who have come a long way on their journey to freedom and being themselves. They will support you on your journey too.

Being You Exercise

People often think that to be an effective communicator, you have to be able to speak well. While this is of course, significant, a large proportion of our communication impact is based on our ability to listen. Think about it; you have two ears and only one mouth!

Step 1. Focus your attention on your heart and mind, tune into yourself with your intuition and the voice within you.

Step 2. Find a place where you can be still and calm.

Step 3. Quieten the voices in your head and the thoughts that run rampant through your brain.

Step 4. Breathe in for seven deep breathes and breathe out slowly and deeply for 11 breathes. Repeat three times.

Step 5. Now, listen to your gut! Yes, that feeling in the pit of your stomach. You know you need to confront it and take notice of it; this is the moment to do that, right now.

Step 6. When it tells you that you are suppressing your natural self and not being true to who you really are and want to be, then listen to that message and really feel it and take action to change your way of being.

Complete this exercise several times to authentically connect with what your intuition and gut is telling you. Be aware of the message they are giving you; accept it and surrender to it. When you know you cannot continue to live your current life, decide on your new path to happiness. The wonderful result that you will be given, after reading this book, is that once you make that decision for yourself, Team Alicia will be there to support you, give guidance and care.

Affirmations

I listen to myself, so I can be true to myself.

I deserve to be myself.

I deserve to love and be loved.

Chapter 3
HEALTH AND WELLBEING

"What I have learned is ... that we need all aspects of life in moderation, not excess; paced, to give us power. "

A dear friend told me she would describe the significant stages in her life by the clothes she was wearing at the time. I said I would describe mine in illnesses and operations! For example, as a baby when I first met my Dad, I peed on him. This could be seen as establishing territory and ownership in an animal kingdom but in reality, it was an overactive bladder! The only muscle in my body that continues to be so active!

Growing up, I had the usual child infections such as measles and chicken pox but I also had an operation to remove my adenoids and tonsils at a very young age. Then, after a couple of years of feeling acutely unwell and losing weight despite eating voraciously (no, child specialist, I did not have Anorexia nor Bulimia) I was – finally - diagnosed as having a hyperactive thyroid at the age of 12! At that time, this condition was unheard of in someone so young, which made me the subject of much research and studies at St Thomas Hospital, in London, United Kingdom. My six-week stay in the children's ward, while groups of doctors poked, prodded and adjusted my medication was the start of a life of generally feeling unwell and constantly balancing medication.

I put off having my thyroid removed until I was 18 years old, as the hospital directed until I had gone through my school examinations and started University. Years later, after having to take the pill daily to stop the totally debilitating periods that rendered me almost unconscious, I was again, in considerable pain and being fobbed off with general diagnoses of – this time - Irritable Bowel Syndrome. It was only by the incredible, good fortune of being recommended to see a Harley Street Specialist who immediately declared that I had rectal Cecal Appendicitis. He put me in hospital immediately - before I died - thanks to the poison that had been pouring into my system from a leaking appendix! Yet more toxins filling my body and was the cause of a most unusual event later on.

When I was diagnosed with Breast Cancer, I believed it was activated by the shock of my mother dying suddenly from a massive heart attack. I went through radiotherapy treatment, which essentially pumped even more unhealthy chemicals, toxins and energy into my body.

When I thought I was healthy and fit again and loving the beach life of a summer on the French Riviera, the most excruciating pain in my back and chest resulted in being admitted to hospital in Monaco. I stayed for six weeks while they tried to discover the cause for the intense pain that required a morphine drip and my being completely in agony. Once again - nothing was usual or standard - my health was always complex and the subject of medical conferences. Eventually, the doctors discovered that for some unknown reason both my adrenal glands had suffered like an embolism, totally out of the blue and died. At the same time, a lymph node under my arm was enlarged and my blood pressure was extremely high. The lymph node issue, a rare condition called Castleman Disease, seemed to be totally unrelated to the adrenal problem. The high-blood pressure was also most unusual with Adrenal Failure.

My beloved Annette went through a far worse time than me. I was out of it with pain, and only fighting to feel stronger and for my life. She had to endure every day of uncertainty – a constantly changing diagnosis - from cancer to goodness knows what. Test after test, scan after scan and finally the diagnosis to be able to put me on yet more medication - and having to find the balance of it all - with the existing thyroid condition. Actually, it was remarkable that they were able to find out the issues, to treat them and that I am alive.

I am grateful for the wonderful doctors and nurses who have taken time to help me and to think outside the box throughout my life. The changes throughout my life because of unusual illness and having to learn to live with the symptoms and treatment has taught me so much.

What I have learned is ... that I am at my funniest when I am unwell! I see the humour in the moments of bleakness and can turn them into a funny positive. Thank goodness I always have a sense of humour. It is essential. Being able to laugh will always provide a relief in any situation. Health is extremely precious. If you are not well, it is so hard to function. There is nothing more important than being well. I think I always pushed myself through exhaustion and pain to keep going and going. Finally, these days because I do not have the same energy levels, or resources to produce energy, I have had to stop pushing and slow down. Managing my time to be more effective and prioritising are two very important aspects of my life. Learning to say no - which is okay - because it means I am saying yes to what is most important to me and to other opportunities. I am using my energy more effectively as a result.

There are many cliches around this subject, such as, "Don't sweat the small stuff"; and "Take time to smell the roses." From my experience, they are so true.

It does not matter if you do not cross off everything on your To Do List today. But it does matter that you tell the people you love that you love them and you give them quality time. It does matter that you keep yourself fit, and as well as possible. Abusing your body is not a good idea. It tries to help you to be strong. Help it to work as best as it can. Your body is a remarkable vessel. Treat it with respect and care. Treat yourself with respect and care. You deserve it.

The 4Ps Exercise

There are 4Ps, which I teach my students to focus on when speaking in public and on camera: Pitch; Pace; Pause; and Power.

In this context of health and wellbeing, I want you to consider the second P, representing Pace, so it can give you the last P, representing Power.

Step 1. It is so important that we pace ourselves. When speaking, it is not too fast, and not too slow. This applies to the way we take care of our bodies too.

If we burn the candle at both ends, or we spend too much time sitting around and doing nothing, we are unbalanced and either burnt out, or lethargic and immobile, leading to demotivation. Pace when we speak, means that we have to remember to breathe at the end of a sentence because we so often forget when we are nervous, or rushing our way through an experience to reach the end. This also applies to your everyday life.

Step 2. Breathe! Stop talking, stop moving and ask yourself the following questions, writing down your answers in as much detail as you can.

- Why you are running around like a crazy person?

- Are you living in accordance with your values and goals?

- Are you managing your time around your most important issues?

Pace yourself by thinking always about who, and what, is most urgent to you and prioritise accordingly. Always, set your pace of life by living from your values. Be very clear on what they are.

Step 3. Stephen Covey in his book, *The 7 Habits of Highly Effective People* (1989) provides an exercise where he asks you to think about what people will say about you at your funeral.

- Consider the most important people in your life, including your siblings, parents, spouse, girlfriend or boyfriend, teacher, friend, boss, fellow employee, sports coach, for example.

- What will they say about you at your funeral?

- Do you want them to say that you never had time for them, or you were uncaring, not dedicated, thoughtless, consumed with gaining money, ambitious, greedy?

By focusing on how you were viewed during your lifetime, you gain insights into how you want to live your life and how you can pace yourself to live that way. It will help you to be healthy and balanced with all aspects of your life in moderation, and not excess, all equally paced to give you power.

Remember, all communication is a form of sharing. The word derives from the Latin word, *communicare*. When I was seriously unwell, I found that joining a variety of forums on Facebook regarding my condition was immensely helpful in giving me understanding and support. I recommend that you join a group on social media, or in person, when you are suffering from an illness, or injury with people who have the same condition. Sharing experiences, notes about medication, diet and medical professionals who can assist, will help explain your feelings and will remind you that you are not alone. It is empowering.

Affirmations

Without my health, nothing is possible.

The most important action I can take is to take care of myself physically and mentally because otherwise I cannot function, nor can I take care of anyone else.

I never ignore any signs that my body or mind is failing me in some way.

I make sure I live a balanced life, in accordance with my most important values and goals.

Chapter 4

BEREAVEMENT: SIBLING

"What I have learned is ... that there are no words to truly express the loss of a loved one. But we must talk about it and express how we feel."

It was before Christmas in 1974 and I was at the school disco. I was wearing my pink Oxford bag trousers and pink and white knitted jumper over a white blouse. I was so happy to mix with the hard-nut girls who surreptitiously smoked cigarettes and the rest of the throng in the main hall. It felt such an honour that I was accepted in all the various groups. I loved the music. I was carefree. It was the end of term. Christmas was around the corner.

However, it was a surprise when my Dad came to collect me in the car because normally it was Mum's role. As we drove home, he told me we were going to Auntie Ruth's and Uncle Monty's house because my Mum was at the hospital with Leslie, my brother. He had been in an accident. Dad would join her there and I would spend the night with my Aunt and Uncle.

I cannot recall if I asked many questions. I think a numbness descended, which continued throughout the night. I felt as if I was living in a dream and I wanted to wake up and find it was not real.

When we arrived at my Aunt's house, my Mum returned from the hospital because they had sent her home, saying she and Dad needed to sleep while the doctors and nurses took care of Leslie. My parent's voices were hushed and solemn, but I discovered that Leslie had been knocked down by a car when he was crossing the road. He had got off the bus coming home from his Saturday job at Take 6, a men's outfitters store. I remember thinking about how smart he had looked that morning when he left for work. How I had not said goodbye, or told him that I loved him. I also thought of how much I had to tell him about the disco and how excited I had been to do so. What laughs we would have when I could see him in the morning!

However, in the early hours of the next morning, the telephone rang and my Dad and Mum went downstairs together to the hall to answer it. I was at the top of the stairs. It was the hospital. Leslie had died. He was 18 years old and about to go to Oxford University to read law. If I had felt numb before and almost in another universe, it was nothing to that unreality I now felt. My brother, the charismatic, funny, clever, handsome, boy was suddenly gone. Leslie, who filled a room with his presence. My champion. My shield. The person who made me laugh when I was down. The one person who listened to me and solved my problems. The person who from the moment I was born, I was his baby; his Liss; his Lissy. No need for me to have any real worries or cares because Leslie was the person who always led other people and was destined for greatness. He was sometimes cynical and sometimes annoying Leslie, with raging teenage hormones. But always Leslie the brightest light.

I think I cried then. I know I was crying in my bedroom on the day of the funeral when my Aunt Connie came in to see me and told me I must be strong now for my Mum and Dad. I was 15 years old and propelled into adulthood and responsibility, with a huge gap between growing up naturally and being thrust forward. A gap that remained unbalanced for many years and responsibility that I never wanted and continued to never want. This has been one of the ironies of my life – never wanting change nor responsibility – yet, they were always there, profoundly present, but not necessarily a conscious aspect of my life.

After the funeral, I noticed how some people crossed the road to avoid speaking with us, as a family.

They did not know what to say. I understand that now. My Mum did not cry. For a very long time, we did not talk about Leslie. We did not say how we felt. How could we express that there was a deep wound, which had a plaster over it to retain a semblance of normality. Actually, it was so strange for me how from that moment of the telephone call, the world carried on that morning as if nothing had happened, in fact. The milk was delivered. The paper came through the door, with the post. We had to eat. Everything continuing and yet nothing was the same. Nothing would ever be the same, again.

Mum and Dad did everything they could to try and ensure that I did not feel alone. They did everything they could to make me happy. They never complained. They were never were bitter, or woeful. They were incredible and admirable.

As I reflected about my brother Leslie and his achievements, not consciously, but planning to study law at university and wanting to be a lawyer, I could not help but feel guilt that he had died and I was alive. All the waves of grief I suppressed to be strong as my Aunt Connie had told me to be that day. But that huge gaping wound left a scar that was deeply etched.

It took a very long time for me, for the gap between adolescence and adulthood to be reconciled. I am not conscious of when they came together. I only know that after many years, I felt the balance. That I could face the wound and appreciate the scar that was there, but was no longer raw and no longer bleeding.

When we lose a sibling who we love, at whatever age we are, we have a fundamental need to talk about our feelings, to cry, laugh, be angry and let it all out. Never keep how you are feeling within you. Talk about the person you have lost and allow them to live in your memory and your life. Never shut them out, or shut yourself away from your grief. It is a painful, deep wound and it needs to be accepted, acknowledged and understood. A plaster will cover it up, but it is better for you when you take off the plaster, look at the wound and confront it. As you peel it off, a little bit at a time, it will help the scar to be less raw.

What I have learned is … that when there are no words, do not be afraid of being quiet and sitting with the feelings you find so hard to express. Let the waves pour over you and allow them to hit you hard and to then, recede. They will surge through you and you may feel overwhelmed at times. But, like the sea waves on the shore, they will subside.

Acceptance and acknowledgement are powerful tools; helping you to recognise that everything will be different for you, but understanding that you can be whole again. You are different. Give yourself time to rebuild. Give yourself permission to come through the shock, the numbness and go through the motions of major change in your own time. Come out of that relationship with the loved one in your heart and thoughts, giving you the power to honour their legacy and their lives, no matter how long or short it might have been.

Compassion Exercise

Step 1. Understand that people find it really hard to talk to someone who has lost a child, or a sibling because they do not know what to say. This is totally understandable, but you can – actually - express that specific feeling to the person. You can say as below.

- "I feel for you so much, but I do not have the words to tell you and I cannot begin to know what you are truly going through."

- "All I can say is that I am here for you, if you want to talk, or cry, or be quiet, or laugh. I am here, whatever you need."

Face the grieving person and talk to them in this way.

Step 2. An alternative action you can take is to

write to them, following that note up with a telephone call and offering to meet with them. Being with them in person is highly supportive.

Step 3. When you are going through the loss yourself, hold on tight to your surviving loved ones, especially your other children, or siblings. Do not shut them out. Make a point of sharing time with them.

Step 4. Or, if you are now a single child as a result of the loss, encourage other people to talk about your sibling with you. Go to loved ones and know that you can be vulnerable and you can live as normally as before and not feel guilty for doing so.

Step 5. When you are going through the loss, consider grief counselling. This will give you more tools to deal with the loss, or help you find the tools within yourself. Most of all, respect yourself and the way you deal with your grief.

Step 6. Always respect other people for their way of coping with their loss. It is unique and individual for each person and know that – with no judgement – however, they decide to deal with their loss, is acceptable.

Affirmations

I allow myself the time to heal from my sibling's loss, with no limit.

I give myself permission to process all the individual steps of grief, whatever feels right for me.

Chapter 5
BEREAVEMENT: PARENTS

*"What I have learned is ... when you have a
wonderful relationship with your parents, your life
can be much easier because with their confidence and
belief in you, you will have a permanent foundation
of security. Without that, I trust that you have other
people in your life, or a special person who believes in
you, so you can live your dreams."*

I have shared the profound change in my life on
losing my brother. We were both young. When
your parents die, it does not matter if they, or you,
are young or old, the gap in your life is still huge. When
your parents are alive, you are always the child. That
role may change as they become elderly and infirm,
but even so, they are the adults. Coming to terms with
having to care for them and become the responsible
one is hard. Losing them when they die produces a void
which cannot be filled by anyone else. Although, other
older relatives, and people who have known you since
you were a child can become even more important
in your life. They have the shared memories of you

and your parents and can keep those memories alive together; but without parents you are an orphan and the feeling of being alone and without the anchor of their love is immense.

My biological Dad, Barry, died when I was a baby. He was 30. I did not know him. All I knew was that my Mum was left to bring up two small children on her own, until a year later her family introduced her to Alfred. From the moment Alfred saw my Mum, brother and I, he fell in love with us all and that love continued for the rest of his life. For me, my Dad was Alfred, Alfie, Alf and he formally adopted my brother and I, so he was truly and legally our Dad. He was very well read and knowledgeable. He sat quietly reading the newspaper, or a book, while my Mum and I talked. He was loving, funny, caring and very proud of me. When he eventually became ill and was not himself, it was very hard for me to only remember his kindness and good humour.

I remember agonising about not choosing him to dance with at the Country Dancing in my Junior School, instead picking my teacher. The hurt I must have caused him brought me immense guilt. I spoke to him about it before he left us and he did not remember it as a slight at all. I was so sorry if I had brought him any unhappiness because he only gave me deep love and joy.

When he died, I know my Mum felt terribly alone. He had adored her and I all his life, and put Mum high up on a pedestal. He would stand on the doorstep waiting for her to come home if she went out without him. He telephoned if we were away from him, asking when we were returning. When I was living away from my parents, at any time through my life, I always telephoned and he would answer and hand me to my Mum! He always asked her, "How is the baby?" or "What is the baby doing?"; or "Where is the baby?" Even when he was 90 and I was definitely not a child, I was always known as his 'baby.'

After he died, both Mum and I felt a tremendous sadness in the loss of his presence, and his devotion. We had each other, of course, and we spent much time together, which became even more precious. But then, less than two years later, my Mum died from a massive heart attack, totally unexpectedly. We were getting ready for her to come to France to stay with us to celebrate her 80th birthday that year. Although, she had visited earlier in the year and said that she thought she would not be coming again. Her mobility in the 10th Century village where we lived was not good and she was very tired. She did not want me to have to push her up the hill in her wheelchair. I told her I would push her up the tallest mountain if it meant we were together! Little did I know that her thought of not returning, was to be prophetic.

When I discovered her body in our family home in England, I called my beloved and she said it was not possible that my Mum had died because she had completed preparing her party invitations. I have the photo of my Mum for that invitation in front of me as I write. It shows my glamorous, smiling, elegant mum – the queen in her tiara - and the queen of my life.

It was an incredible shock to lose my Mum that way. I was very concerned that it was a shock to her, too and she would have felt bereft of not being able to say goodbye to me and prepare me for her parting. I know that I spent at least two years after she died going through the motions of life. I cried my way through airports, restaurants, cafes and any place we had been together. I felt utterly lost and without identity. She was so much my focus and such a huge influence on my way of being, that – at that time - I could not exist without her.

It took me a long time to realise that to honour my Mum and Dad and to keep their legacy alive, I needed to find myself and be the person they had given me the strength to be. That all my life with them had given me the courage to be me – always their daughter - and always anything that I wanted to be.

What I have learned is ... when you have a wonderful relationship with your parents, you are truly blessed. And, even if you don't, this chapter can still help you. One of my dear friends knew how I was floundering when my mother died. She told me to, "Put one foot in front of the other." This wise advice helped me to get through the many days and months of my grief, when I did not seem to be present and I felt as if I was sleep walking my way through life.

When your parents die, you are for the first time in your life truly the adult in your family and the responsible person. It is a void and a big gap that cannot be filled by anyone or anything else. It makes other people in your life who have known you for a long time even more significant. Those shared memories and history, are so important because they make you the person you are today.

The only way to deal with the grief and manage your loss is to live your life to the fullest and to be the best that you can. Live it with joy, love and cherish all the good and beauty. Be grateful for all that you are and all that you have. Through time, the sadness reduces and the pain is less acute. You never completely come out of the fog that envelops you when your parents die because life is always different after that major event. You are changed. But that difference and change will enable you to come into your own and stand on your two feet, knowing that their lives were for a purpose and reason and so is yours. The best action you can take is to honour them and continue their legacy by being everything you are; by being authentically you.

Heal Your Heart Exercise

Step 1. To heal from any loss, whether through death, divorce, or the end of a relationship, you must first accept the reality of the loss.

Step 2. However, many people are in denial at first. In the initial stages, you think the person will be coming back and they are only out, or away for a period of time. When the reality kicks in, you realise that you are not able to physically talk together, or see them anymore. It is at that point, that you work through the pain of the grief, by adjusting to life without the deceased and maintaining a connection with them, while also moving on with your life.

Step 3. Recognise that you may feel any of the following:

- shock, disbelief, numb, denial that the loss has occurred;
- sadness, despair, loneliness, emptiness;

- guilt, regret, shame;

- anger, resentment;

- anxiety, helplessness, insecurity, fear; and

- physical symptoms, such as fatigue, nausea, sickness, weight loss or gain, aches, pains, night sweats, heart palpitations, feeling faint or light headed, and insomnia.

Step 4. It is normal for you to feel any or all of the above. Know and understand this honestly and realise that you may need to take time out to work through your feelings, which is perfectly acceptable.

Step 5. Tell your support group you need more help.

Step 6. Do not grieve alone. Stay connected with other people during this time. Talk about the loved one that you have lost. Tell someone about the circumstances of their death. Do not be afraid to share the experience.

Step 7. Confront any guilt you may be feeling. Perhaps, what you did or didn't do while your loved one was alive, or guilt about not feeling 'sad enough' or moving on while your loved one is dead. Let go of the guilt and commit to living a life that will honour the deceased.

Step 8. Write your feelings down, or say them out loud to yourself. The best way is in front of a mirror, which allows you to recognise the feelings and let them go.

Step 9. A helpful and practical action is to be creative to express your feelings. Paint, write, or create a scrapbook, photo diary, or play a musical instrument and sing.

Step 10. Alternatively, take physical actions, by taking a walk in the fresh air, or doing exercises outside, and feel the elements of nature help clear your head and focus on the beauty of nature.

Step 11. Eat and sleep well and do not feel bad for doing that, even if it means for a while you indulge in comfort food, a little! Nothing to excess or extreme!

Step 12. Imagine your deceased loved one in a chair in front of you and express whatever you need to say to them, as if they are there in the room with you. This is especially helpful if you feel there is unfinished business between you to resolve.

Affirmations

I am patient with myself and the other people around me who do not understand what I am going through.

I take one day at a time.

I feel joy and hope again in my life.

Chapter 6
ABUSE

"What I have learned is ... that buried emotions
will manifest and rise to the surface. The key is
not to bury them back down but confront them; to
understand them at a deeper level. Doing so leads to
healing and freedom of spirit."

My family was always loving and affectionate. Totally giving and supportive. We always talked with each other. If I could not express something to my Mum, I told Leslie, my brother and he would tell her. After he died, I spoke to her directly and my Dad. They were always there to listen, although most of my communication was with my Mum. I knew Dad cared and gave advice and I will never forget how he was incredibly open, strong and clear in any situation or tragedy, or when I was changing my life.

When a prodigal family member arrived in our house when I was a young girl – maybe 10 or 11 – returning from abroad after many years away, I expected him to have the same secure, caring and stable qualities as the rest of my family. He was someone, though, who gave very little but expected adoration from other people all of his life. He received it from all women who seemed to be charmed and besotted by him. Personally, I did not see the appeal. I found him rather creepy. I had a feeling that I did not want to be around him, which of course turned out to be true!

I recall that I was in the bathroom when he came in. He shut the door and asked me to stand with my legs apart and he touched me in my private parts. It was uncomfortable and I felt really awkward. He told me to stand still and he kept touching me. As I write this, I feel sick. It is actually really hard for me to get the words out. But I feel I must express this event in my life to protect and help anyone else who has to go through a similar trauma at a young age. I am sorry that I cannot tell you how long this episode went on for. Eventually, he left the room and I washed myself, stunned as to what happened. I could not bring myself to talk about it for at least a day or so. I avoided him and locked the door of any room I could without drawing attention to the fact that I had done that. We were not a household who normally locked our doors.

Then, I told Leslie what had happened. He said he would like to kill him and that I must tell Mum. I could not face doing so, but I don't remember if he did it for me, or insisted that I did. All I know is that when I confronted my Mum with what my relative had done to me, she was dismissive. She did not make anything of it, as if it was nothing. I think she said that he would be gone soon and we would not have anything more to do with him.

What I have learned is … that it was abuse from a trusted relative. And that memory has stayed with me all my life. I have not been able to face it, or let it go and I have suppressed it. I urge you not to do that. Nowadays, there are so many places and helplines and people who you can tell and talk it out with. I do not understand why my Mum dismissed it. Now she is no longer alive, I cannot ask her. I could not find the courage to ask her when she was here. Maybe, she felt that by doing so and making it out to be nothing, it would not be so significant for me. Maybe, she was too stunned by it to know what to do. Maybe, he had been abusive to her, I would not have put it past him! Whatever and why my Mum responded the way she did, I have learned that it was not correct. I trusted him. I certainly trusted my Mum. He took from me, in that moment; he stole an innocence and belief. No-one has the right to do that to anyone else.

I often wonder if my feelings of threat from men generally in my life has stemmed from that incident. I was powerless. I have met so many women and men, who have suffered abuse in my legal career and subsequently, in my communications training, and coaching. I have worked to protect these people and to give them a voice and the power to express themselves, with confidence and clarity, to explain situations of intense emotional impact, so they can regain control of themselves. In writing this chapter, I am actually completing the healing for myself, too. My relative was in the wrong. Any abuser is. You are not. It is their inadequacy or their issue. You cannot help them. You must help yourself. Any abuse – physical or mental – is unacceptable and intolerable. You do not have to take it. And if you do, know that you ultimately have the power because no one can take away your light and your love. These will shine through and give strength to other people to come through the darkness.

Reclaim Your Power Exercise

When you have suffered physical or mental abuse, you need to reconnect with your body, soul and personality to reclaim your balance and personal power. You need to reclaim your reality, heal your brain and act from a place of empowerment rather than trauma.

Step 1. I have always been told to meditate and I always found it immensely difficult to do so! However, I am aware that the benefits are bountiful, especially if you need to mitigate the fight or flight responses that go haywire after a trauma. So, bearing in mind that I have not been able to do this well, I can suggest that you find your way of meditating. Maybe, listen to a guided meditation on YouTube, or other sources. Or, take a moment before you go to sleep, to ask for healing from your spirit guides, or from loved ones. Lay in bed, with your eyes closed and feel the healing energy flowing through your body. Or, go to a meditation class or one with yoga. This will combine mindfulness and physical activity to restore balance and bring empowerment. The effects are scientifically proven to be very powerful in easing depression, anxiety, increasing resilience and bolstering self-esteem.

Step 2. Take physical exercise, but gently, so you can return to having a relationship with your body. Research has shown that doing yoga increases self-mastery and rebuilds a sense of safety that abuse robs from you. Paying particular attention to your breathing engages your body and mind in a purposeful way and resets your brain, which has been disturbed by the trauma. I recommend yoga or swimming, or Tai Chi or any movement exercise where you are focused on breathing and moving in a gentle way, calming your soul, as well as your brain.

Step 3. Self-compassion is essential and the

most powerful form of compassion. Treat yourself with understanding and sensitivity. Every day, say compassionate mantras, such as:

- I am worthy of true love and respect; and
- I deserve peace and I have the right to express all of my feelings and to feel them.

Remember not to judge, nor blame yourself because you are worthy of care and kindness. Always work on yourself to change the course of your negative self-talk.

Affirmations

There is an empowering life ahead of me after physical or mental abuse.

I can survive and thrive.

I am committed to my self-care.

I never give up hope.

I always have control of my thoughts, my voice, and I can think myself away from any situation.

I speak and live my truth.

Chapter 7
STUDY

*"What I have learned is … to talk and communicate
with other people and to find the friends in any new
situation or environment, who will be your friends
forever. When life is new and uncertain, they will
help make your life bearable. They will support you
and show you the way forward."*

L*ove Don't Live Here Anymore* (Rose Royce, 1978)
was playing when I walked into the Students
Union at Warwick University, England. The
floor was sticky with beer and the air was foggy with
cigarette smoke. These were my first impressions of
where I would be studying Law and Sociology for the
next four years of my life.

I had not thought I would go to university and I
had really enjoyed my summer holidays job at what
was then the retail shop, British Home Stores. I started
in the Lighting Department and within six weeks was
promoted to a supervisor. Six weeks after that, I was
promoted to a pay point controller, which I loved,

including the camaraderie, contact with the public, and managing people, sales and money. So much so, that I applied to join the Personnel Department or Human Resources (HR) as it is called today. With the support and backing of my store manager and the HR director, I went for an interview in London. As soon as I stepped out of the elevator, and was greeted by my interviewer, I knew I would not get the job! I sensed that she felt threatened by me and she did not want me in the company. I was right! Much to the surprise of my store manager and team, I was not hired. This was one of the first times I learned that women in business do not - or did not then - unfortunately, support each other!

My plan B was to accept the Warwick University place offered to me after I interviewed there. Mum and Dad took me to the campus and settled me in. Mum had made chocolate cake so I could take it into the common room and share it with my new accommodation mates. However, when my parents left and I watched them drive away, I felt very sad and alone. This was my first time away from home and a whole new way of life. One where I had to manage my time, finances, studies and establish new routines, find new friends and remember to eat, without the support of my incredible parents and my friends at home. Did

I feel overwhelmed and lost? Yes, I certainly did! For a start, I had to find out where my classes were and then work out how to learn everything that was being taught to us and submit work within the imposed deadlines. I also needed to find time to enjoy myself! To take in the culture offered, including the theatre, music, films, and disco!

Learning to live a more communal life for the first year especially was not easy for me. Sharing a kitchen, toilet and bathroom between a dozen people in the campus accommodation was so different to anything I had experienced before. Fortunately, as my culinary skills were none too great, nor my time management to shop, cook and eat, I was able to enjoy my meals in the cafeteria. That was a great asset for me because it not only gave me sustenance, but also time to make, sit and talk with new friends.

Time was a balancing act. Making the friends who have remained with me throughout my life was wonderful. It gave me support to study and to continue with the degree, when I felt like giving up after the first term. I was homesick. I remember crying down the telephone to my Mum on several occasions, putting my money in the old pay telephone on the stairway of the accommodation (no mobile telephones then, either). I did not feel confident enough in class to speak up and it was challenging to cope with the work load, which was far greater than I had ever been exposed to before. For that first term particularly, it was all new. Unlike many of the other students who loved this opportunity of freedom away from their parents and family, I did not know how to stand on my own two feet.

What I have learned is ... that it is necessary to be disciplined. When faced with a totally new situation and environment. When you learn to study as is necessary for a college or university, or are learning aspects of a new job, or you are retraining, always give yourself structure. When you are given assignments, construct a timetable or schedule to fit in study time and give yourself breaks. I always spent an hour studying and took a ten-minute break. Make a cup of tea, or coffee, or look at your texts or messages, or social media, and then go back to work. Or, go for a walk, and enjoy the fresh air. Make sure you schedule time to talk to family and friends and to do pleasurable activities. Also, deal with the work as soon as possible. Never put it off. The more you put it off, the more you cannot face it.

Always meet new people and talk with people in your new situation, or on your course, or at clubs or groups that you like to be involved with. Although, remember never to join too many groups because you will be overwhelmed. If you are studying online, or going through retraining, again meet people who are on your course, or studying in the same way, so you can talk and discuss what you are going through, and study together. Having a 'study buddy' can be a huge support.

Also, never be afraid of expressing your difficulties. Tell your tutors. Tell your teachers. Never be hard on yourself if you do not understand what they are talking about! Be patient with yourself and other people. Give yourself time to find your new way of learning, living and being. As in all things, be true to yourself. If after you have given yourself time to settle, to learn and grow, you still feel it is not the place for you, then walk away, knowing that you have tried your best and it has led you to where you should be. I stayed at Warwick for the full four years of my course. After the first term and the first year, it became easier. I learned to enjoy the culture and appreciate the opportunity. I was determined to complete my degree with a good grade. I urge you to be determined and dedicated to achieve your goals. Stay focused.

Plan Your Week Exercise

You will need a diary or calender with you for this exercise. I recommend a diary with a weekly page, so you can fill in the daily slots, week-by-week.

Step 1. On a Saturday or Sunday, fill out the diary for the week ahead placing the most important tasks that you have to complete for your studies in the days ahead. Firstly, your lectures or meetings, which are scheduled already. Secondly, any essay that has to be submitted by the Friday of that week. Allocate time each day to write that essay around your scheduled lectures and meetings. If another assignment is to be completed the following week, see if there is time in the week ahead, after you have filled in the urgent task, to spend time on that assignment, as well, placing it in the diary.

Step 2. Complete the diary for the week, filling out time for your most important activities, including: time to spend with or communicate with a loved one; to do food shopping; to complete life administration tasks; sports; walks; and exercise. I recommend that you build into every week, time for physical activity. I found it very helpful to work for an hour or two hours and then have a break of 10 minutes to walk, or enjoy the fresh air outside. By doing so, you are making your schedule in accordance with what is important to you and also necessary for your studies to be completed on time.

Many of my students have found it overwhelming and hard to keep on top of their work, because they have so many places to refer to for assignments and schedules in these days of online platforms. By keeping a diary, or weekly planner for yourself, you can go to the schedules for your courses, at the start of every week, as well as keeping a note of what is urgent and important for you. However, never beat yourself up if you do not stick to the planned schedule, but try always to face the tasks that you least want to do because you will find they are actually much easier than you have contemplated! Ultimately, your life can be organised by your most important and not urgent tasks because you will be living in balance and harmony.

Affirmations

When I am studying in a new environment, or retraining and having to learn new skills, I am disciplined, organised, but always make time for me.

I give myself structure and stay focused on the study I have to do.

It is only for this period of my life and it will give me so many more skills.

I am committed to it, without losing sight of myself in the process.

This study or retraining is developing my abilities and giving me a broader outlook.

This study or retraining can bring me new friends and opportunities.

If I find, however, that I do not enjoy it, or it is not giving me satisfaction or fulfilment, then I am not afraid to step away from it.

If I step away from this study or retraining, it has taught me what my most important priorities are and I say yes to these instead.

Chapter 8

JOB, WORK, CAREER

*"What I have learned is … that change and
disruption have become a part of our daily life,
especially when it comes to our work. Rapidly
evolving technology, an ever-growing amount of data
and the need to integrate globally, make it hard for
even the most forward thinkers to survive all the
changes and the need to manage it and capitalise
on it. We all need support and understanding.
And we need to work out of love and not fear,
collaboratively."*

When I left university, I went to the College of Law in London to compete my final law examinations, to qualify as a lawyer. Or known as a solicitor, which is an English word meaning a lawyer who appears in some courts and instructs a barrister to represent clients in other courts. I trained for two years with a firm of solicitors, before qualifying. But actually, I joined a lawyer who was setting up his own practice and in fact, we ended up setting up a practice together and hiring four staff. This meant I was thrown in at the deep end, conducting all types of law, including: criminal; civil; family; litigation; wills; and probate. It was a very steep learning curve, rather than spending time in each separate department of a larger practice and being able to absorb the knowledge and experience. However, within two years, I was a partner in the firm and we had more than 100 staff and other lawyers working with us. Within four years, we acquired two other partners and I was working incredibly long hours and became totally exhausted.

I changed law practices several times, never really having good experiences at any of them and I never honestly felt that I was good at the work. Not having had the chance to learn from established solicitors, with a structured learning plan, rather than getting on with it and learning on the job, I always felt I was inadequate and lacking in knowledge. I always felt that my fellow partners undermined me, although they appreciated that I brought in new clients and I looked after those clients very well. But I always felt useless in their presence because of my insufficient training.

When faced with leaving the last law practice altogether, without keys to the office and all my files, or continuing from home, with my Mum as my secretary and my Dad as my accountant, I decided not to lose the goodwill I had established and all my clients I had worked so hard to build up. I set up on my own and slowly and gradually, my clients found me and came to me, bringing their families and friends. It was a huge step and a massive gamble for me, but it was also the best time of my legal career! For the first time, I was doing what I loved most about in law, which was helping other people with problems and without the feeling of anyone looking down on me and judging me with criticism and negativity.

Later the same year, I met my beloved and started coming back and forth to the South of France. I decided then that I would not be a lawyer, or work in the law when I moved to live with her because I was so tired of being in an environment which was stressful and frustrating. I loved being able to help people but the constraints of the law were difficult to handle. That led me to working, firstly, on the radio, secondly, in events, and thirdly, having my own internet television show, before I finally found teaching, in fact coaching, training and teaching in communications. Again, I was helping people, which is my purpose but without the exasperation of having to work within a limiting system controlled by other people.

What I have learned is … that for much of my working life, I was undermined and treated without respect. I dreaded going into the office and having to deal with my partners, let alone the work load. There was pleasure in truly being able to help and guide people through terrible times in their lives. Their appreciation kept me going. However, the pain of not being in an environment where I was supported really took its toll on my psyche, as well as my wellbeing.

When you wake up in the morning and you dread the day ahead - especially your working day because you are not following your passion and you are being thwarted by your colleagues, your boss or your manager - it is time to make a real change! Think carefully about your role, answer the following questions and write down your answers in as much detail as you can.

- Are you working at what you truly want to do?

- Can it be different for you?

- Can you do different tasks within the job that you have?

- Can you communicate what changes you would like to see in the organisation?

- Is there anyone who you can talk with, to consider alternative ways of working?

- Can you step away and set up your own business, follow your dreams and only do what you love?

Change Your Thinking Exercise

Albert Einstein famously said; *"We cannot solve our problems with the same thinking we used when we created them."* Let's take steps therefore, to change your thinking!

Step 1. Know that you have a voice and you can use it. Things will not improve if you keep fighting the existing reality. Make a new reality! No matter what your work is, involve everyone who works with you or for you in constructing new models for the way the company operates. Talk with your managers, your staff and your boss and share your vision. If you work alone, use your social media, or contacts to help brainstorm and develop your plans for a new reality.

Step 2. Take ownership of and responsibility for the change by providing training programmes, or being involved in training that will take the company and you further in developing new ways of behaving and operating.

Step 3. Lead, manage and embrace change. See it as an opportunity to create a better working environment for you and all of the organisation or company and everyone who will be involved in the process.

Step 4. Collaborate and empower! By communicating through social media, as well as other forms of communication, give your employees the chance to lead their followers with new ideas. Encourage them to voice their understanding and interpretation of what is essential to cope with the changes occurring or that need to happen. Recognise who are your leaders and empower them to do the job. Or feel empowered yourself to engage and create dialogue.

Step 5. Take your time and build steadily, slowly and surely. Use your imagination, and visualise the picture of what you want to see happening in the change. How it can be managed, then materialise that image by filling in the details, step by step, steadily building.

Affirmations

When I follow my heart, I will be where I want to be in my head and in my life.

I focus only on what excites me, inspires me and what I truly love.

I know my purpose in life and make my decisions only based on that.

Chapter 9
MOTHERHOOD

"What I have learned is ... that when you want to have children and for some reason that has not happened, you can still give your love to children, animals and other people. You can be loving and love, without condition and with fulfilment and happiness. Your role as a mother and satisfying your maternal instincts can be achieved in other ways."

There was a time when I wanted to have children. I had no idea of what being pregnant would be like, or carrying a child and giving birth. But I wanted to nurture my child and pour my love into it. But that was not to be. My husband and I had different views on bringing up children and they were not compatible. I do not regret that I did not give birth to a child. I never have regrets. Whatever happens in life is for a reason. It brings you to where you need and want to be. I thought it would have been lovely for my Mum and Dad to have grandchildren, but I spoke to them about this and they did not feel any loss. They were happy to have time with me, wherever I was and whatever I was doing. They actually felt some relief that I did not have the worry of bringing up children in an ever-changing world. And I felt the same. Would I want my children to have to go through all the concerns I had experienced growing up with more pressure in society today?

Some people consider it selfish if you do not have children. They think that you are not fulfilled, or complete. How can you live without giving life to another? As with everything, it is your choice. You can decide if bringing another person into the world, caring for them, supporting them and letting them live their life for themselves and not for you, is what you truly want. In any event, you can have other children in your life and be a nurturing presence.

I have been blessed to have my soul son in my life. He is not physically mine, but our bond and connection are deeply attuned. I am certain that we have been together in other lives; and in this one we are here to love each other without judgement. I have learned that I am here for him, to give him the reassurance, understanding, security and peace that he needs. He has taught me that I can do that and he will always give me the same. I do not expect anything from him and without expectation, he will be totally giving. Our lives often run at a parallel, which is so often a revelation, when it is really not a surprise. I have come to realise that he is never away from me because I know how I am in his thoughts and heart, as he is in mine. I had to learn that in letting him live his life as he chooses, I am truly letting him live. He knows I will always guide, advise and support if he needs it. He also knows that I will be proud of him beyond words and accept his foibles without judgement.

There have been several friend's children who I have had the blessing to spend time with and receive tremendous affection, as well as be able to influence and give counsel to. Now, I am a teacher of students, young and older – a huge pool of children - to nurture and help. The joy in watching all of these children grow and mature and to follow them as they embark on their adventures, is profound. All the better because they are responsible for themselves. I can listen and learn from them.

What I have learned is … that being a mother can be in different forms. You do not have to physically give birth to a child to have an effect on their life and be able to help them follow their path. You can be very present in a child's life, which will give them joy and enable them to flourish. The 'Aunt' or 'Uncle' who is there for other people's children, to spoil them, pamper them and treat them is a gift indeed! Giving them your time and listening to them is so important. Being able to be objective with them can be a great asset. Sometimes you can be the bridge to their parents when communication is not so easy between them.

Live Your Best Life Exercise

These steps are especially helpful to teach the children in your life, as well as being applicable for adults.

Step 1. Live your life to the fullest.

Step 2. Be there for anyone when they need you.

Step 3. Value the importance of self-worth.

Step 4. Provide food, shelter and love.

Step 5. Make time to have fun.

Step 6. Allow mistakes to be made and learn from them.

Step 7. Realise there is no 'should' or 'should not', when it comes to being a mother or not.

Affirmations

I can be a great influence in my life and be incredibly loving, even if I am not a mother, nor have my own children.

It is my choice whether to bring children into this world or not.

I can be powerful in so many other ways and make an impact in the world.

Chapter 10
RELOCATION

"What I have learned is ... the art of patience and not losing hope. Finding a new country to call home and living in a different place is daunting, but it is also exciting."

Why would you change your whole world by moving to a completely different country and culture?? Why would you disrupt the life that you are comfortable with, that is known to you, and familiar for a life in a different country where you do not speak the language, the culture is totally different, there are new people and different food? Or maybe that is why; for the challenge; to start afresh; to be a different you; or to be the real you.

Many years ago, I visited the South of France on holiday and met two South African ladies living there. That meeting changed my life. From that first conversation in a coffee shop in the back streets of Cannes, I came to visit the Cote D'Azur regularly and was introduced to the love of my life through those fabulous women. It took 17 years before I moved to Roquebrune-Cap-Martin, but during those years I learned to adjust to a new life and all the changes that brought.

At first it was very hard. I was lonely. I felt isolated and vulnerable because I was reliant on my beloved for transport and all of my life in a foreign place. Okay, I was fortunate that she was there and had a life rich in experience, but I was used to being independent. I needed work, friends, products I was used to and I had to cope with the administration issues of France. Plus, the feelings of homesickness for my known life in England and the people who I loved there, all of which was sometimes overwhelming.

As with everything in life, making new friends, finding your place in a new community and talking, talking, talking in the language of that country really helps. The only way to learn the language is to speak it! Yes, I went to French School, which introduced me to people who started my own circle of friends and helped me to start conversations everywhere with the people who lived and worked there. For me, having friends, contacts and acquaintances helped me enormously because I felt supported, understood and I knew I was surrounded by people who had either gone through the same experiences, or were going through it with me.

One part of my freedom and independence was to have my own car! To be able to drive anywhere I wanted to go and not be reliant on public transport, or anyone else was a big deal for me. Driving on the other side of the road to what I was used to came incredibly naturally. It was also really important for me to work in a different career than the legal profession I had been involved with in England. It was all part of the new and different me; free to be myself in every aspect of myself. I took on work as a personal assistant to a person who turned out to be a rogue. But then I found a lasting friendship with someone who established an events management company with me, until he moved away. After that, I found my vocation in teaching, training and coaching. Never could I have dreamed that I could have found the perfect match for my skills and my life's purpose. However, the hardships of finding work and losing work; finding friends and losing friends as they came and went from the country, which was such a transient place, also took its toll. Dispondency, elation, confidence, security and lacking in self-belief and feeling lost; all were the roller coaster of my emotions.

What I have learned is … how important it is to immerse yourself in the culture, and learn the local values and customs. Appreciate the small things. But never expect that it will happen in a day. Take the time, knowing that you have the time to develop your new persona, or enhance your old one. Be open to new experiences and new people. You may find you go through several jobs, relationships and time when you think nothing is moving you forward, but it will all bring you to where you need to be and how you want to be. Believe me, I am here, now.

For example, once when I went for a medical test, the nurse said my accent was charming and she could not believe that I was speaking French so well after having only lived here full time for around five years. That appreciation gave me such a boost! I add this story as an emphasis of how persistence pays off and sticking to the path of immersion in the life of the country you relocate to. You can make the change, rather than allowing the change to demotivate and lead you to feel dispirited.

Communications Exercise

Changing your home to another country means you are learning a new culture, as well as possibly a new language. You may have many miscommunications by making assumptions - never positive - because broken down the word 'assumptions' means making 'an ass of u and me!' This exercise will help you to deal with potential miscommunication, and not to assume.

Step 1. Never judge other people in your new location negatively, if they behave differently to you. They may not act in the same way as you are used to. That does not make it wrong. It makes it different. We send and receive wordless messages by body language, eye contact and facial expression. Your new home and country may have a different use of these aspects.

Step 2. As in any communication, know your audience. For example, I conducted an interview with a Japanese student once and she did not look at me the whole time. At the end of the session, I mentioned she had not looked up at me throughout and asked her why. She said that in their culture this was a mark of respect and deference to me as her superior and she was in awe of my presence. I had thought her rude and disrespectful and had wondered why she was looking down the whole time!

Step 3. Learn about the culture and customs of the country, as well as the language. Know that even two countries that seemingly speak the same language, have different words, or meanings for words. I am married to an American and even though she has lived in France for more than 30 years and I have been with her for 24 years, when we speak English together, some words are pronounced differently and may have another meaning! For example, the word 'pants' means 'underwear' for me and 'trousers' for her.

Step 4. Listen; such a wonderful communication tool! When you listen effectively, you will be able to immerse yourself in your new country, or new environment. That means you listen with all your senses like the Chinese word *Ting*, which means to listen with your ear, mind, eye and heart. Use your ear to hear the words; your mind to understand the words; your eye to observe non-verbal messages; and your heart to understand the feelings of the speaker.

Step 5. Learn the language if you can. It really helps to be part of the place where you live and to feel that you belong. Even if it is only a few words, it gives such a boost to your feelings of being involved and settled.

Affirmations

I create a totally new me in a different environment, shedding old habits and patterns of behaviour.

I experience wonderful new adventures and embrace the change!

I learn the language and culture and I never make comparisons with my previous location.

Chapter 11
AGEING

"What I have learned is ... that life is precious. We spend so much of life doing, rather than being. We forget that we are human beings, not doings! It is always so much better to be satisfied with what is happening in the present moment, in the now."

As you mature with years, marks appear on your face and body out of the blue! You look in the mirror and you do not recognise where that line, or wrinkle, came from, or the hair poking out of your chin and your nose. You glance at yourself in the window and you think it is your Mum staring back at you! Your knees go saggy. Weight appears on your midriff and thighs, until you are in your 70s and 80s when you simply cannot eat as you once did. Only half a sandwich and not a whole one and no crisps. You feel like you are may be transparent because somehow you have become invisible to other people who do not look at you in the same way. They look through you. The changes are imperceptible but real.

As a child, everything is possible. No fear. No worries. Any concerns can be shelved, or put aside. Life is ahead and is an adventure to be explored. As a teenager, reality starts to kick in. You study, you start a job. You have a relationship, you have sex. You want to be popular, look good and the pressure starts. Problems seem insurmountable. In your 20s and 30s, you establish yourself in a career, partnerships, and maybe motherhood or fatherhood. The pressure to succeed and to achieve grows. In your 40s, you begin to feel comfortable in your skin and more established. In your 50s, maybe you change direction, with more time for you and your relationships, rather than focusing on your children. You feel more secure in life. In your 60s, you are more content, appreciative and grateful for what you have; not pushing anymore nor being so driven. In your 70s, you feel the aches and pains even more when you move your body. In your 80s, you are far more conscious of time speeding up and moving incredibly rapidly, with days, weeks and months disappearing. And beyond – hopefully – when you are grateful if you have your faculties, mobility, security and independence.

As you mature, it seems that time moves so quickly. When you are young, you feel that days are long and a summer holiday will last for weeks and weeks. Later, any holiday time seems to fly by. Just as you are relaxed from the usual deadlines and stresses of everyday life, it is time to return to them! Every ten years brings different priorities. Your attitudes change. What was important as a 25-year-old is not as relevant as a 50-year-old. Experience gives you an insight into what is really essential, and what can be re-focused. As a 20 something, or 30-40 something, you are ambitious; you are quite selfish and think only of yourself. As you get older, your attention is to being well, loved, content and at peace. Plus, pursuing the activities you like to do and want to do, rather than have to do. Fulfilment is different as you age. You have achieved so much and lived through so many experiences that it is no longer about accumulation.

What I have learned is … that when people urge you to live in the moment, they are right! Instead of wishing your life away impatiently when you are young, make the most of every day to be where you want to be, enjoy your youth, agility and everything that stretches ahead of you. Cherish each minute. Every age is allowing you to grow, develop and learn. Acceptance is critical and knowing that each age has its merits. Never fight against it. One day, you may not be able to do as much in a day as you did when you were younger. It does not matter. What is so necessary for you to do it anyway? Always keep alert. Keep active. Keep stimulated. Spend time with people of all ages. Listen to them. Talk with them. Share your thoughts. Age is only a number. You can regard it with trepidation, unease and anger. Or, you can embrace it, enjoy it and always feel that lightness of being a *Dancing Queen* (Abba, 1976).

DISCO Exercise

This exercise focuses your attention on the following impactful actions.

- D = Discipline;
- I = Imagination;
- S= Selflessness;
- C= Concentration; and
- O= Observation.

Step 1. D: it is never too late to be disciplined with yourself and to take care of your body. Walk as much as possible and exercise daily. Look after your teeth! We so often forget when we are growing up how important they are! Keep them clean, white and hygienic! Regularly, take time for you. Eat well, sleep well and rest in between activities. Follow a regime that will benefit you in later years and keep moving! Dance, run, ride a bike, practice Yoga or Pilates, or Chairobics, swim or enjoy that Zumba class.

Step 2. I: imagination is wonderful to keep your brain stimulated. Be creative. Think outside the box. Imagine yourself being exactly where you want to be now and not in 20 years time. See yourself there now and picture yourself there now, so you will be there, now! Imagine all the possibilities of life and keep those thoughts in your mind, every day.

Step 3. S: being selfless and thinking about other people will help you to stay young and vibrant. When we communicate, it is never about us – it is how we want the other person to think, feel or do - as a result of our communication. Thinking in this way whenever we speak, or talk and hold a conversation will help us to stop focusing on ourselves and by giving, we will grow with wisdom and maturity.

Step 4. C: Concentration is aligned to discipline. Being focused and in the moment, will stop us from wishing life away and enable us to live the age we are. Concentrate on what is the best for you now. Concentrate on your goals and values and focus on the priorities for you.

Step 5. O: when you are observant in life, you will always have something to talk about and think about. It ties in with selflessness – when you observe people around you and compliment them when they change their hair style, or wear new glasses - for example, you will not only make them feel recognised and acknowledged, (something we feel less of as we age) - but you will also feel good in yourself. And, take time to observe the waves on the shore, the moon in the sky, reflecting on the water, the leaves on the trees and in doing so, you will be grounded, balanced and calm.

Affirmations

I can learn, grow and develop myself in every period of my life.

I embrace the challenges that every 10 years brings, with wonder, enthusiasm and passion!

I believe that every age brings me more insight, maturity, wisdom and joy.

I face ageing with excitement, as I did when I was a child.

Chapter 12
DEMENTIA

*"What I have learned is ... never to berate yourself
for the times you are impatient with a loved one
suffering from Dementia. You are human and your
frustration is as real as theirs. Never focus on the
memories you remember, but they do not. Live in
the present and do not look back. They may have
a fabulous recollection of the years gone by, but not
what they had for breakfast, or what they need to
do to lock the door. Listen to their stories and do not
force them into thinking about more recent events."*

My Dad, Alfred was a gentleman. He served
in the Royal Army Pay Corps during
the Second World War and attained the
rank of sergeant major. He was always immaculately
dressed, with shoes polished and sporting a tie most
days. Indeed, he never wore a T-shirt and only in later
years, put on a polo shirt because it had at least, a
collar. He was funny, loving, devoted to my Mum and
I, and Leslie my brother, and one of the most well-

read people who I have ever known. When Leslie and I were growing up, Dad knew where to find the answers for our homework in books, rather than the Internet. Alfie, my Dad, played sports with us, taught me how to play snooker, of which he was a champion player and was always kind, caring, full of optimism and generous to us and all our family and friends. He was the accountant for my law practice when I set up on my own because figures, accounts and numbers were his forte, as well as his profession.

When he started to behave out of character, or deeper into his character traits, like his unwillingness to be without Mum by his side, in an exaggerated way, we were a little concerned. I say a 'little' because it was such a gradual deterioration that we did not think too much about it at first. Dad could lose his temper, but he had a very long fuse, so when he became cantankerous and shouted and was swearing, even in company and out of the house in public places, we became very worried. He seemed to go off in this way for no apparent reason and it was very hard to calm him down.

He was also very obstinate; refusing to go into a wheelchair when he could not walk without difficulty and swearing and shouting abuse at us for trying to force him into the chair. Until, he decided one day that he would sit in the wheelchair and then we could not get him out of it! Eventually, he was diagnosed with

Dementia, after many temper episodes. Also, he could not remember anything, leaving doors open and food cooking on the stove. He had always been an excellent cook and suddenly he could not recall how to turn on the oven.

There are so many examples of how he was not the same person, but it happened so gradually that we could not identify at first what was the issue. He also became very hard of hearing and we thought initially when he seemed to be in another world and absent from the conversation or what was going on around him, that it was because he could not hear. Certainly, that was the case early on, but then he would focus on young children and babies and be absorbed with them. It was almost as if he had reverted to being a baby himself. It became clear that he could concentrate on his surroundings, but he was not able to express it or only in a very limited way.

I am glossing past instances of his behaviour being embarrassing and painful to witness, because I do not want to remember my Dad like that. I do not want to face again those last days of his life, when we had to take him into hospital and when he begged us not to leave him. But he could only speak about numbers and going through accounts because that was all he could manage in his head. I want to give you a picture of a person who was suffering with Dementia, but I want to keep in my head and heart, my Dad who was clever, witty, fun and who adored me, cared for me and put Mum and I first in everything he did.

I was often frustrated, intolerant and impatient with my Dad when he could not behave in the way I had always known him to. It was hard for me to continually tell myself that his anger, or his inabilities to function were not his fault and he was not himself. That the Dementia had seized control of my Dad and taken him over. I also felt incredibly sad to have lost my Dad while he was still alive. And I felt sorry for him that he could not fight against the condition because I know he would never have wanted to live as that person he had become.

What I have learned is … that Dementia is a serious and horrible disease. Sadly, one that has no cure at the moment. My Dad was in his 80s when this started to happen for him, but it can be diagnosed at any age. It does not make it any less painful if your loved one is young, or elderly when it happens. You lose the person that you love, slowly and surely, even though they are still alive. But they are still with you and you need to accept that while your relationship will change, you can still love them and care for them with gratitude for all they have been to you when they were without the illness.

Recognise, too, that everyone in your family will respond differently to the deterioration in your loved one and the way they deal with it. Be tolerant because everyone's relationship is different. Very often, your loved one does not know that they have Dementia and this is a blessing. Think of the blessings, like the good times you have shared and do not let the pain and sadness tarnish those.

Use of Language Exercise

Firstly, think about your use of language when caring for a loved one who is suffering from Dementia.

Step 1. Never use words such as, "Do you remember?" They cannot remember and it will make them sad, as well as you. Talk about shared memories, but their recollection, not yours.

Step 2. Get into the shoes of the person suffering. Try to see the current situation and their life from their perspective. See their world as it is now, not in the past and not in the recent present. Be in the moment with them now. Their world has changed and will not go back to how it was. Try to create new moments of happiness and joy for your loved one in the world they inhabit now.

Step 3. Build structure for your loved one according to their structure, not yours. If they made a cup of tea in a particular way, follow their example. Do it as they do and understand how it works for them. Follow how they prefer to order their lives because putting new systems or processes in place will be unsettling and disorientating for your loved one. Think about how you might put food on a plate, for example and how you serve that food. There is a sequence to what you do. For the person suffering with Dementia, they have lost that ability to sequence, but they still have an awareness of how it should be and it can be disturbing for them if it is not as they performed it.

Step 4. Keep routine and structure, but always with the understanding of the person's minutiae.

Step 5. These diseases are a living grief. You are losing a part of your loved one over a period of time. It is a form of loss for you, be patient with yourself, as well as the Dementia sufferer. Know that facing the vulnerability in someone you once viewed as strong and powerful will take time to come to terms with. Do not feel incompetent. Give yourself time and space to feel whatever emotions come your way and know that what you are feeling is normal.

Step 6. On a practical basis, being the former lawyer that I was, always have a Power of Attorney legal document prepared, signed and in place while your loved ones have the ability and mental capacity to grant this power. It will make life much easier in a potential future situation when the person is no longer capable.

Affirmations

I accept that I am losing a loved one to Dementia and the changes that have occurred in that person and our relationship.

I am grateful for loving this person and I stay present with them, always.

I create joy in the world while we are both alive now.

When they are no longer here, I will think about them as they were at their best and of what we did together with deep love and affection.

Chapter 13
PANDEMIC

"What I have learned is … that whatever is going on in the world and however bad … it is always best to appreciate all the positives in your life. Rather than focusing on what you are not sure of, concentrate on what you know. That you have love, laughter, the sun, the moon, the flowers and the sea."

In the year 2020, Covid-19 came into our lives suddenly and unexpectedly. From being free to travel and socialise, to being affectionate and demonstrative; enjoying theatre, music, dance, working together; being at school together and being in crowded groups together, we have been in lockdown. Socially distanced; wearing masks; unable to touch and hug each other. Loved ones have been taken ill and we have not been able to see them in hospital. We have been parted from the people we love, with concern for their health and that we could bring infection to them. The world economy is suffering. The whole world is affected. It is a global phenomenon, without cure, as I write.

Whether you believe the situation is a political conspiracy, or you believe that it is a real disease that can kill people, our lives – during this year 2020 - have been changed beyond comprehension. Children who normally run freely with their friends can no longer be close to them. Teenagers leaving school, or older children leaving college and university are faced with finding work, or continuing their study in an unrecognisable world. Work is generally online, from home. Education is online. The way we communicate is different. All these online platforms that were useful if we were not able to meet in person, are now the norm because meeting in person is the exception.

This is a true story that does not have a conclusion yet. The effects on our mental, and physical wellbeing in the long term, are unknown. In the short term, we know that people are suffering from stress, anxiety, uncertainty and depression.

Personally, the time in lockdown was very busy! My teaching and training went online and though it was incredibly stressful at first to use the new online platforms and to work with them, it was good to be able to be proactive. It was also heartening for me to be able to help and support other people with their communications in these different times.

I was able to work from home with my sweet heart

Contact The Author

Please contact me via my website, as below, and let me know which experiences of change you have embraced and how the chapters about those challenges have helped you the most. Please share your experiences with me and how you have used the communication exercises to support you. I am always delighted to receive your feedback and comments, and to welcome more change communicators into Team Alicia.

Also, please contact me for personal coaching and training in communications, and for your company, foundation, association and organisation.

Website: www.aliciasedgwick.com

LinkedIn: https://bit.ly/AliciaSedgwick

Facebook: https://bit.ly/AliciaSedgwickFB

YouTube Channel: https://bit.ly/AliciaSedgwickYT

Printed in Great Britain
by Amazon

55618781R00068